SPEAK AT SEA
FOR FREE

Three Ways To Turn Your Talents
Into Worldwide Travel

If you have dreamed of traveling the world, there is an opportunity for those with the skills to educate and entertain to fulfill those dreams on a cruise ship. Enjoy the benefits of cruising by trading your wisdom and expertise for free travel worldwide. Read on!

By Nancy Soulé
http://nancysoule.net

CHAPTER 1
Your Passport To Paradise

Take a moment… Imagine yourself sipping a piña colada on the sun-drenched deck of a magnificent cruise ship, the Caribbean breeze wafting through your hair, the warm sun caressing you—not as a paying guest, but as the featured speaker who is there for free? Did you know that you may have the opportunity to utilize your particular expertise and turn it into your passport to paradise? But be aware – ya gotta know your stuff – this ain't a "free ride."

Every year there are more and bigger cruise ships being built to cater to the 66.2 billion-dollar cruise travel industry. What if you could tap into your wealth of knowledge and experience, those many years of honing your craft, and use it to allow you to travel the world for free? Are you a speaker? Do you have a wealth of information on a particular topic that you're anxious to share? Maybe you have a hobby at which you excel as an expert? Do you like to travel? If you fall into any of those groups, you may be an ideal candidate for the sought-after, and exclusive position of "Enrichment Lecturer" on a cruise ship!

Ships offer a unique opportunity for a multi-generational vacation that provides a one-stop-shop for luxury accommodations, culinary delights, and a wealth of entertainment, all while exploring various exotic ports of the world. Ship's crew must entertain hundreds to thousands of people in a captive space, and for days on end. Most often, there are one, two, or three sea days (or possibly many more) between ports of call that require intricate scheduling to keep everyone engaged. And a repositioning cruise, a temporary change of home ports, may have no stops at all and last for many days as they cross the Pacific, the Atlantic, the Mediterranean, the Caribbean, or even from one ocean to another. As of 2025, more than 323+ ships (and the number changes every year) are sailing the Seven Seas at any given moment, hosting 37.1 million passengers. That's a lot of people to keep occupied and entertained. The ships do their best with their cruise staff to host games, trivia on a wide array of subjects, Bingo sessions, dance classes, dance parties, theater and comedy shows, scavenger hunts, craft challenges, etc. These are primarily hosted by onboard entertainment crew. However, there are numerous opportunities for noncrew passengers, people with skills, talent, and engaging ideas, to participate in these sea-day offerings by providing additional alternative special event presentations on a variety of subjects. That's where you come in!

CHAPTER 2
What? They want me?

I discovered this opportunity to become an "enrichment lecturer" quite by accident. I had been performing as a musician and vocalist with a local blues/pop band in San Diego, and had no clue about how to get booked on a ship, but I wanted to try it. I went to the library (back when the internet was in its infancy) and looked up the corporate address of one of the big cruise companies. I bravely assembled my VHS tape and photos and sent them off with big ambitions and great anticipation. Besides performing in the band, I was also an instructor for a fashion college, so along with the band promotional materials, I also included a little trifold brochure about a presentation I occasionally offered called *"The Seven Secrets of the Wardrobe Wizard."* I had used it to appeal to women's organizations to promote my clothing and wardrobe consulting business. The response I got from the cruise line was much different than I expected! I was tremendously excited to get a response, but actually, they had no interest in the band (little did I know that specific agents were responsible for that and I was completely "barking up the wrong tree") but they were more intrigued to see the *"Wizard"* do her magic.

They referred me to a booking agent who managed the paperwork, and I was contracted for a seven-day Caribbean cruise in late May! I would not actually be paid and I had to pay my own airfare, but the cruise would be free; and this was about a $3,200 value! I flew from San Diego to Miami with a girlfriend as my assistant. I packed waaay too much, dragging heavy suitcases of demonstration materials and supplies. We were afforded a cozy inside guest cabin on a Norwegian Cruise Line ship. Our free cruise adventure took us from sunny Miami to Barbados and St. Maarten and back to Miami. In the course of the week, we enjoyed the magnificent beaches as well as the historic island sites. Onboard, I was expected to present three events, for which each had a different aspect of the general topic.

On Day 2 of the cruise, to start revealing the *"Seven Secrets of the Wardrobe Wizard,"* I donned the elaborate royal blue and silver beaded wizard robe and pointy hat I had made, waved my magic wand (a light-up, star-topped rod I had found in the toy department for aspiring fairies), and began the romp through the first of my three presentations.

Number One was about personal style and how to determine which shape of clothing aspects would suit each particular body type to emphasize the best parts, camouflage the lesser parts, and flatter the figure. Broad shoulders and no butt? Big butt and sloping shoulders? A big box? Super curvy? A round ball? Ok, I was certainly more genteel than that, but you get the idea.

The next was all about accessories: how to choose hats, from crown size to brim shape; use scarves to cover, add color, or become a part of the outfit; choose flattering earring styles, shoe styles, etc. Accessories, jewelry, and shoes can make or break an outfit and finding appropriate shapes, styles, and colors to flatter the user's proportions is crucial to creating a balanced look. Staying current with fashion trends can determine whether you look hip or frumpy. And colors that are appropriate for your skin tone always create an impact. Whether for leisure or business, these elements can sometimes make or break a first impression or even a business deal.

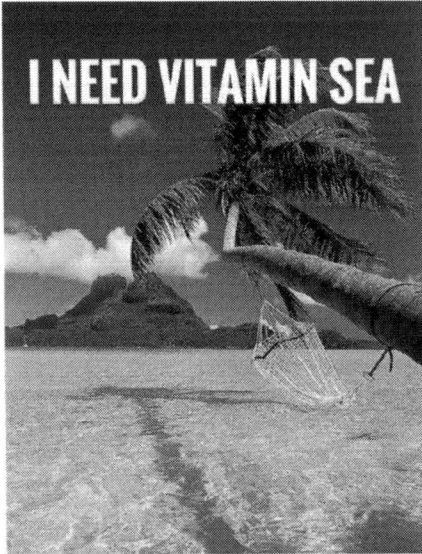

The third session was called "*What's New and Is It for You*." I had slides (yes, the real ones in an actual carousel projector) of the high fashion designer collections from Paris and Milan. We examined all the crazy ideas and fascinating presentations of the haute couture runways and scrutinized how to pick out the bits and pieces that would most likely be translated into ready-to-wear collections and what the guests might expect to see trickle down to their local department stores.

I had interactive demonstrations along with the slides, a plethora of wardrobe accessories that I could try on various guests, and I did my best to "edu-tain." The room I was given for my presentation was near the lunch buffet and I was set to go at 1:00 pm on three sea days. This arrangement created a ready audience to start with! It was up to me to keep them in the room past lunch, and entice them to come back on subsequent days (which they did!). Granted, the men seemed to drift away after the meal, but the ladies were entranced.

Apparently, I was a hit with the guests as the cruise line was very pleased with the comments. As a couple of wild and crazy single California women "on the loose," I have to admit, my friend and I flirted outrageously with a cute bartender and a sous chef, and could have gotten them (and ourselves) in serious trouble if we'd gotten too carried away. Fortunately, we generally behaved ourselves, but a magnificent plate of chocolate-covered strawberries was most unexpectedly delivered to our cabin! Once back in Miami, we rented a car and extended our stay a few days to maximize the vacation. We explored the famous South Beach and dined on the waterfront as the parade of locals and tourists strutted by in all manner of attire... or lack thereof!

CHAPTER 3
Making it Count

At the time, I didn't have a business to promote that would relate to a remote clientele, the internet was kind of a "new thing," and I didn't think to secure or maintain contacts with event attendees. These days, if done respectfully, and not blatantly, one might be able to utilize the opportunity to obtain contact information for later interaction via QR codes, digital cards, and free offers. Each company has different requirements, and some will allow you to sell your books or products in their gift shop. They typically retain 20-30% of the sales price. It's not a "back-ofthe-room" arrangement, as your presentation is *not about you*, remember it is all about the *cruise guest experience*. You are there to make the company look good and "enrich." Your product is not there to be touted, just allowed to be available should there be interest.

The benefits for your hours of preparation/presentation are huge however. The actual cost of the cruise for you and a traveling companion can be gratis! Some lines may cover air costs, but not all, and certainly not for your traveling companion. You may bring anyone with you that you choose as your room is double-occupancy. Someone can come to assist or just join you for the adventure. Depending on your experience and your booking agent, your first time out may be arranged as an "audition" cruise for which you might be asked to cover your cruise costs as a regular guest. The ship will put you into the activity schedule and assess your performance which will be reviewed by management as well as the guest comments. Should that process go well, thereafter you may be invited back without charge. If you are fluent in other languages, and depending on the cruise itineraries, that could also offer opportunities for a variety of other presentations.

If you have never cruised, it would be wise to experience one to understand the procedures onboard and get familiar with the intended type of audience. It would also allow you to get familiar with the types of venues available. Should you be concerned about the "motion of the ocean," bear in mind that today's cruise ships are a completely different experience from the transports of the past! No longer are passengers subject to the whims of the ocean so much, with the broad beam of the ships, the mechanical stabilizers, and the numerous navigational tools installed to mitigate whatever turbulence may present itself. If storms are on the way, the ship just goes somewhere else! Port schedules have to be kept flexible as the weather may dictate a change of itinerary. Today, ships are their own destination with swimming pools, hot tubs, and water slides, some with bumper cars, video game arcades, iFly skydiving air tunnels, and even ice skating! But should there be a need, eating green apples, ginger, and downing some Dramamine can help. Be aware, Mother Nature always has her surprises.

CHAPTER 4
How it works

Depending on your experience, the company, and the itinerary, as a "newbie," on your first trip (that "audition cruise,") you might be asked to pay for any cabin you choose. But based on the comment and presentation results, that second opportunity will be different. You will still be given a guest cabin, but most likely not in your first choice of location, you may not have a balcony but rather be assigned an inside cabin, as you are a non-revenue guest. There is often an onboard allowance for discounts in the gift shops and bars for purchases, and maybe even for shore excursions. The additional cost of mandatory cabin gratuities may be discussed/negotiated with your booking agent (more about agents later.) You'll be treated like any other guest with full cabin attendant service, and you can enjoy all the live music, theater entertainment, pools and hot tubs, and massive amounts of food. You are free to explore all the amazing ports of call. Usually, port fees and taxes are covered as well. The booking agent can clarify the details and relevant costs.

Be aware, however, that there are personal costs involved for you for which you need to be prepared. These my include:

1. A valid passport for all those who are traveling, with at least six months available past the expiration date. If there are visas or vaccinations required, be sure that information is investigated and be prepared well in advance.
2. Transportation to the embarkation port for both you and a companion (whoever you may choose).
3. Hotel accommodations for the night before sailing to ensure punctual arrival with allowance for airline delays, weather, baggage issues, and time zones.
4. Onboard gratuities (mandatory) which can range from $15 to $20 per day per person that must be secured either by credit card or cash at boarding. Later on, with more experience, some agencies may be able to negotiate these on your behalf.

5. Cash tips for airport shuttles, hotel assistance, cruise port luggage porters, taxies or ride shares, and extra onboard gratuities such as room service.

Depending on the itinerary, these **three or four one-hour presentations** can potentially be a value to you of $1000 to over $6000 in travel perks. If you are booked **on a 14-day cruise, you may need five or six offerings.** Once you have been officially approved, the options to continue are tremendous. Not a bad return for your time. Wherever you want to fly in the world, if your subjects are appropriate and time is available, you're in. Ask your contact at the cruise line after the trip for a copy of guests' comments, or circulate your own evaluations as part of your presentation to use for ongoing booking validations.

CHAPTER 5
What To Do First

So, are you excited? How do you make this happen? If you are not (yet) a professional speaker, don't worry. You may not really have to be. You just need to be an "expert" on your topic, be able to speak with presence and authority, and be able to answer any relevant questions. Here are some tips to help you out.

10 elements that will make your presentation shine:

1. Have valuable and/or interesting content; KNOW YOUR STUFF!
2. Be well researched
3. Be well spoken (use appropriate grammar, be succinct)
4. Be clear, use your "storyteller voice" with volume and melody
5. Be well prepared and rehearsed
6. Be organized
7. Be entertaining (humor goes a long way; just keep it family-friendly)
8. Be personable and interactive
9. Be ready to answer questions
10. Be professional and gracious to all onboard, guests and crew alike

Before you dive into the plan, determine your ultimate goal. Is this adventure just to get "a free cruise?" Remember, that "free" cruise will have those associated costs (time, transportation, hotel, food, etc.) for just getting to the port and back, especially if you are taking a co-cruiser. And if you're not fully prepared and the presentation doesn't go over well, that's the end of the road; you won't be back. So, determine what it is you want to accomplish in this endeavor. Some cruise lines might cover your airfare, but not the flight for your companion, and some may also require a COVID or other vaccination or a booster (ask your agent.)

Consider your prospective audience, and be mindful of your most appropriate target age range. Do the guests on this particular cruise line suit your demographic? What is the predominant nationality on your itinerary? This is information usually available from your agent. Some companies are more senior/retirement focused and often provide longer cruises (maybe a circumnavigation of Australia.) Others are shorter, weekend/minimal time-off-work itineraries (think Los Angeles to Ensenada and back) for the younger, working set, and others are more focused on family vacations and have prioritized leisurely days at the beach. The primary idea is to provide educational information that is both useful and entertaining. There is a wide variety between cruise companies and their requirements of you as a speaker.

University-type lectures are not appropriate. You're there to inspire, and certainly not to bore them. Your session should be fresh and entertaining as well as informative. You will be rated by the passengers on each cruise, and if you score well, you will be invited back. As an instructor or workshop host, you will be required to adapt your programs to fit into the schedule defined by the Cruise Director, and that will vary by cruise line.

As mentioned before, passengers may range from the elderly to families with children. Those that patronize the more high-end cruises are primarily in their 50s to 80s. They expect to be both entertained and educated beyond their already high level of sophistication. They have many choices for their leisure time activities, so a speaker needs to be dynamic, with great visuals, and be able to speak extemporaneously; don't just read what the audience can already see on a PowerPoint slide. The presentation should appear to be spontaneous, without just reading notes, be very informative, and especially entertaining.

A comparison between the biggest cruise in the world in 1912 vs. the biggest cruise in 2013.

As you well might imagine, given the benefits, the role of Enrichment Lecturer is a very competitive endeavor, especially for newcomers. Unless you are a well recognized speaker or instructor, you need to be prepared to impress the corporate shipboard "enrichment managers" that the agents may be contacting on your behalf. They will want to see a brief and relevant profile/CV/bio, as well as a short video clip that shows your presentation style and some samples of your content. This "sizzle-reel" should be approximately 10-15 minutes in length and can be edited to highlight the best segments of your full program. A list of past presentation organizations or speaking opportunities should be included. Remember, you need to have at least three, probably four speeches prepared. They can be uploaded to YouTube, or another online platform, that can be accessed via a link. The booking agents can guide you through the process for what sort of content is most desirable and their preferred format.

Once enrolled though a booking agency and accepted, some will provide an online portal or distribute a list of open ships, dates, topics, and itineraries to its speakers. Others may require a more intensive initial personal interview from which they can recommend you directly in response to the lists they have of requests from the cruise lines. If there are specialty cruises on the books for which a particular subject should be addressed, you can be top of the list if your presentation suits the requested criteria. After your first gig, if you like the teaching/cruising life, and the cruise line approves your performance, you may be allowed to request back-to-back cruises or more specific itineraries.

CHAPTER 6
Give It Time

Bookings are typically done 8 to 18 months out, so don't be in a rush. However, once proven, you could possibly be needed in as little as a week prior if you are experienced and known to them, if there is an occasion where there a short-term opportunity is available. Typically, however, you have plenty of time to prepare. If the company is one that will cover your air transportation, they may prefer to book you on a route closer to home so as not to incur extensive travel costs. As a newbie, declining an offer you receive may make it difficult to secure another booking. Give it a try even if it is not your first choice of itinerary. If you have a particularly hot topic or are well-known, however, you may have a bit more leverage. Let them know beforehand if you have scheduling restrictions such being unavailable during a school year or have pre-arranged other obligations. Cancellation is not typically an option and can destroy the agent's inclination toward further offers.

Speakers and Instructors also need to be active in applying for opportunities themselves. With most agents, nobody is going to call you up and offer you an engagement exclusively without first getting acquainted and noticed. Once in conversation with a booking agent, stay in contact to let them know of your willingness and availability. For some of the mainstream lines, the agent does not typically determine the appropriateness of the speaker/program for any particular ship or cruise line. Some may provide online access to a listing from which the cruise company representative may select subjects and speakers from their postings, and they can determine which presentation will suit their clientele. That company rep can then contact the speaker directly (that's how I secured mine.)

The decision as to who a cruise line engages for any particular cruise is in the hands of the enrichment booking manager at that cruise line. They will consider your profile, suitability, and your unique proposal for each cruise. The agent does not usually have any influence in that decision and serves to recommend. Nor can they provide you feedback as to the progress of any application you make via the agent's platform.

According to the advice from CruiseShipEnrichment.net, "Each enrichment booking manager at a cruise line will have their own selection criteria depending upon the enrichment program they want to offer for a specific cruise. There would be no such thing as the 'best' candidate for any particular cruise, unlike what one would expect with a career-type job with a salary. Cruise ship speaking and instructing falls into the realms of Onboard Entertainment & Enrichment and as such the enrichment booking managers will probably be thinking about how a particular candidate can fit into that program. It would be impossible for us to give advice as to how any one candidate could make themselves "better" than another candidate. Every speaker and instructor's act is going to be unique."

Each cruise line enrichment booking manager will be reviewing your application and will take into consideration your submission for the cruise, as well as view your profile and any showreel attached. Hence it is important to have a strong profile and a video showreel to make a good first impression. And remember, not everyone can be successful with every audition. Every cruise line engages different types of speakers and instructors, has a specific clientele in mind, and there is no set rule. Sometimes there are "specialty cruises" booked by various organizations and those may entail certain relevant speakers. Having intriguing and interesting presentations, especially on a topic of current or unique interest, may entice bookers to take special note. Especially if you are an engaging and entertaining speaker who can hold the attention of an audience. It's always an advantage if you can bring them to genuine and spontaneous laughter! After all, they are on vacation!

For some of the higher-end lines, the agent might be the one recommending you personally to the line as you have been thoroughly vetted, and they are confident on the high standard of your offering and skills.

CHAPTER 7
What companies are looking for speakers?

Agencies represent the opportunities onboard most major cruise lines such as Crystal, Royal Caribbean, Celebrity, SilverSea, P&O, Holland America, Regent, Carnival, Princess, Disney, MSC, Norwegian, Viking Ocean Cruises, Cunard, etc. Virgin Voyages, Villa Vie and Ponant are lines that don't often express a request for speakers. Some other, such as Viking or Regent, are booked years in advance. If you are interested in being listed for availability, you may apply to the agencies listed herein. Be well prepared with the information recommended here to maximize the contact and endear yourself to them. Be clear as to your background, skills, and presentations, and your availability and flexibility for booking.

As you consider any offering that may be presented to you, bear in mind that if you are not a seasoned cruiser or even a local boater, this is an adventure on a ship. Even though it is actually a floating city, the ocean often has a mind of it's own and Mother Nature always gets her way. Depending on your itinerary, you may be relatively stable on the ships that stay generally close to coastlines: Alaska, the St. Lawrence Seaway, the western coast of Mexico. But even there, the winds blow, the seas swell, and you may experience some turbulence. Crossings of the Atlantic and Pacific are a bit more challenging, and by all means, be aware that the hurricane season (June 1-Nov 30) in the Atlantic and Caribbean may create some modifications to itinerary, or circumstances where you may have to ride out some temporary rough weather. Ah, the joys of cruising. However, be aware that whatever the scale of a storm, the ship's captain is cognizant that whatever may be coming, there will be a decision made about how to avoid any discomfort or hazard to either the guests, the crew, or the ship. Either way, know your own tolerance for motion, and bring your remedies to be prepared.

Once onboard, you are acting as a representative of the company. Some cruise lines may limit your participation in a few of the onboard activities. These may include participation at the gaming tables in the casino, sitting at the open bars, or carrying a drink when walking in public areas. On others, they realize you are a professional, and can count on you to behave properly, so they may offer to comp you for expensive shore excursions or tours in the ports of call!

CHAPTER 8
The 3 Ways to make this a reality;
Ready to go for it?

Here are the three basic categories to consider in developing your presentations. You should be prepared with <u>at least</u> **three to four 45-minute talks**. They can all be from one category, or a mixture of different ones. If they relate to each other, there is a greater potential for repeat attendees. Extra points if you have interesting PowerPoint slides, fascinating videos, special "show-and-tell" materials, or exciting interactive exercises to make the event visually appealing and more participatory. Room sizes and participant numbers may vary depending on your presentation content. Every cruise line usually has different criteria for what they deem as appropriate for their clientele, so one speech may not translate between cruise lines. Consider these options:

1. **Destination relevant**- One of the most sought-after roles. Typically hosted by those who are well traveled, be sure to research the itinerary that you are considering and examine whether you have knowledge and/or expertise regarding the history, the native culture, indigenous people, industries, music, language, or the geography/geology the area. Maybe you can offer some essential language skills for local communication in a foreign country. Much of the extra information you can find online to augment your already extensive knowledge on the subject. With some cruise lines, Destination Speakers are also required to promote the port excursions, so familiarity with the region is invaluable.

Examples:

- Language skills with basic communication skills for languages such as "hello, thank you, I love [your country/city/town/shop], good morning," are especially helpful in countries where English is less frequently spoken, and is of tremendous assistance in experiencing the local culture for friendly basic communication. French, Spanish, Greek, Turkish, Arabic, Hindi, Swedish, Finish, Chinese, Korean, Japanese, etc. are valuable to any traveler. Consider your itinerary and skills. A bit of research on the history of the language and local dialects is also of interest.
- If there are historic events that happened in the destination locations such as battle sites or strategic forts, their history and significance can be highlighted. Particular city events for which the region is noted, such as fairs or

celebrations can be explained as well as presentations about the associated cultural costume or significant parade floats as relevant. Think Mardi Gras…

- The tremendous history of the many geological events (volcanoes, hurricanes, glacial changes, etc.) can be explored that have affected the location's population or geography and left an indelible mark are great topics, such as Mount Etna, Mount Vesuvius, and Stromboli in Italy, Mauna Loa and Kīlauea in Hawaii, and Mount Fuji in Japan. Other important volcanoes include Mount St. Helens in the United States, Mount Kilimanjaro in Tanzania, and Mount Pinatubo in the Philippines. The changes that have happen among the various cultures as a result are relevant. Tsunamis, floods, etc. have a way of changing everything.

- There are numerous sites worldwide of ruins left from past civilizations such as the Pyramids of Giza in Egypt, Machu Picchu in Peru, Angkor Wat in Cambodia, and Chichén Itzá in Mexico, and of course Pompeii and Herculaneum in Italy among many others. These sites offer glimpses into the past, showcasing the ingenuity, power, and cultural achievements of past societies. The mysterious building techniques, and the impacts on humanity are relevant.

- Some other subjects of interest are the specific port's history or politics, as well as gastronomic specialties such as local food and wine. Other regionally specific instruction or background may be provided on such social activities such as Greek or belly dancing. These can provide an opportunity for interactive and culturally-relevant insights.

- Naturalists who can talk about the flora and fauna of Alaska and its everychanging glaciers, and meteorologists who can and provide visuals and answers for the phenomenon of the Northern Lights are always of interest.

- The volcanic activity and geological history of the Hawaiian Islands can provide terrific stories of the earth's history. And throw in some Hula in the mix as well as native language exposure to enlighten the visitors about the local history and traditions. Paleontology experts can reveal discoveries with fascinating peeks at the earth's history and creatures; dinosaurs anyone?

- Engineers may be impactful by explaining the history, politics, construction, and drama associated with the enormous endeavor of building the Acropolis, the Pyramids, the Panama Canal or other constructions at the ports of call such as Rome, Piza, Florence, Cuba, Athens, Toyko, Singapore, etc.

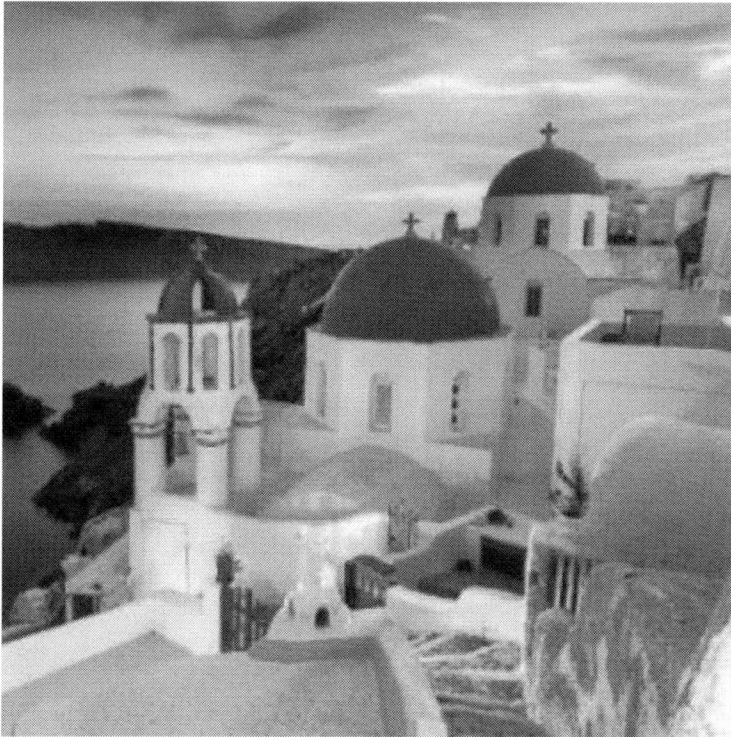

Santorini, Greece

2. **Crafts** - These are more relevant to the mainstream lines and family-oriented cruise itineraries. Choose an activity for which you have expertise, skills, or a passion that is relevant to the itinerary. It should be something simple, easy to explain, require easily transportable supplies, be applicable to a variety of ages, and easily completed in under an hour's time. Often the company will have a monetary allowance for "educational materials" to defray some of the costs of supplies if you have them prepared and itemized for their approval beforehand.

- Creative writing or memoir preparation,

- Needlework,
- Paperfolding/origami,
- Macrame (sailor's knots!)
- Instruction/history of the game of bridge or other card games.
- Balloon twisting,
- Face painting,
- Drawing,
- Painting (be especially conscious of maintaining a tidy space so as not to damage the presentation space or the company's furniture.)

3. **General or specialized interest** - Something that appeals to a variety of nationalities, age groups, and education levels are always in demand. Avoid political or religious subjects (just like common advice for any dinner party) and make it exceptionally fascinating and hopefully useful and relevant. Sometimes scanning the list of best-selling, non-fiction books may provide some ideas. Maybe one of the following will spark an idea.

General Interest:

- Biographical information on famous/popular historical or currently relevant people
- Language skills are always useful in foreign ports;
- Photography using your cell phone or basic improvement procedures or equipment recommendations for cameras;
- Meditation of various types;
- Physical/mental improvement such as fitness and anti-ageing;
- Business skills: motivation, management, and marketing ideas (bear in mind, these folks are on vacation and most probably don't want to think about work);
- Dancing: so many types (ballroom, country, ethnic dance); ☐ Magic or basic slight-of-hand.

Always consider your audience, their interests, their ages, and also their capabilities (see the crafts section above).

Special Interest Topics:

- Various members of the clergy, particularly rabbis and priests, are in demand, especially for religious celebrations or regular meetings. Some folks may request a wedding official for a specific religion.

- Astronomists, especially in times of predictable celestial events are valuable resources for understanding the skies above. Similarly, oceanographers can enlighten guests about the tremendous and various mysteries as well as the challenges that face our oceans and provide opportunities to reveal new discoveries and enlighten people about atmospheric changes. Similarly, Space and aeronautics can be relevant topics, especially when sailing out of ports where there are launches in close proximity.

- Historians who specialize in the history of 20th-century cruise ships and ocean liners, are sought-after onboard speakers. I know of one gentleman who has spent 40 years studying every aspect of the events and people involved in the voyage, and ultimate sinking of the Titanic. His four lectures, with full PowerPoint slides, focus on the building and sailing of the vessel, the passengers' histories and families, the numerous films that have been made throughout the years, and the changes to maritime law and procedures that have been instigated as a result of the tragedy (any why we're all safe now!)

- Art History can augment the information often provided onboard by the art gallery. Park West, the provider of original artworks and prints for purchase onboard may appreciate a more in-depth look at any of the particular artists that are featured for sale, or general art appreciation.

- Interesting creations such as the architecture of Fank Lloyd Wright, Frank Geary, or other visionaries have left impressive structures. If there are architectural marvels in the itinerary's ports of call, those would be of particular interest to augment tour guide's information.

- The Crown Jewels and other shiny objects are subjects covered by a certified diamond grader, for example. However, she leaves the discussion of the details of the purchase of diamonds to the onboard sales team.

- Another in-demand topic is forensics, spurred by the popularity of such TV shows as "Law and Order" and "CSI," so anyone involved in the field or in a famous court case may be of interest as a speaker.

- The history of classic movies is another idea: the musicals of the 1940s, the old contract system of hiring in Hollywood, particular themes like the works of significant directors such as Hitchcock, Scorsese, Houston, etc.

or secrets of the careers of famous movie stars, musicians, or exceptionally famous bands are often fascinating.

Scour your particular abilities and find what gets you excited to share as your enthusiasm will be the pivotal factor in your presentations. The booking agents will be invaluable in helping to refine your ideas. Be prepared to represent yourself as an "expert" with years of experience to back it up. Take the time for careful and succinct preparation of handouts or follow-up procedures for audiences to connect with you later for free information such as access to your presentation slides, a list of tips to help them use your information in their lives. This is not a sales pitch, but an informative opportunity for education and entertainment.

Tap your skills, education, experiences, and achievements. Be ready to provide a variety of programs as ship schedules can often fluctuate based on weather and unforeseen circumstances. If there is time to be filled, and you can provide a solution to their anticipated "down time," the cruise director will be eternally grateful! It is always a good idea to keep them happy. These presentations are nearly always on sea days, and the ship staff will be very supportive in providing whatever equipment you need such as projectors, screens, audio/lighting support, etc. to make you look good and facilitate your presentation.

Sydney Harbor Australia

CHAPTER 9
Essential things to know

As in any professional relationship, remember these things:

1. Always be prepared in advance to advise the staff in advance regarding any set up that is needed, and they will accommodate you.
2. Always arrive at the port a day ahead of embarkation to ensure a timely boarding (often you choose an expected time; come early.)
3. Notify the cruise director immediately upon arrival so they are aware that you are onboard, you are ready, and you are prepared.
4. Be engaging and entertaining, both on stage, and off. You are posing as a representative of the company, and remember, you are there to make them look good. If you have any complaints, direct them only to the cruise director in private. You didn't pay for this cruise, after all!
5. Always arrive to your venue at least 15 to 30 minutes prior to your presentation time to confirm set-up and sound check.
6. Your performance may be recorded for post-presentation broadcast to guest cabins.
7. Your assessment is based on company evaluation and guest comments. Never complain, you are there on their dime, so please be cordial to everybody! Graciousness and gratitude always go a long way.

CHAPTER 10
Who ya gonna call?

So, now that you know what to do to be prepared, how do you get in front of the right person to start this new adventure? First there is some research to do. Clarify your subject matter. With some ideas as to your desired plan, the best avenue is to contact some agents (see the list that's coming soon as a start) and explain your interest in being what is commonly termed an "enrichment lecturer."

Be well prepared with **a list of titles and subtitles, and with very brief (two-to three sentence) summarization of each presentation,** offered with clarity and precision. Be ready to explain why you are an expert in this field. They are busy people and will be making a quick decision as to whether your topic may be of interest to their guests. Be cordial, professional, and courteous. Don't be offended if they tell you something you don't want to hear. They know their clientele, so respect their feedback. Some may charge a small fee to be listed with them as it takes time and effort to put together your profile on their platform. Others may charge an administrative fee for each day a speaker is placed on a cruise. Some may have an online portal where you can easily communicate and see the potential offerings.

There may be a "set-up" fee, and/or a subscription change to access the agent's listing opportunities. That portal is where your personal profile, showreel, CV, or other information will be posted for the cruise lines to peruse. Depending on your representation, some agents may promote you, while others don't, but rather provide access to those who are searching. You can access this portal profile to promote yourself to other organizations that may be in search of your presentations. The agent will guide you in the creation and setup of your profile. They are familiar with the companies, their itineraries, and the guest demographics. If you have prepared the information as outlined here, it may save you some time and money to simplify their processes and they can get you onboard more efficiently.

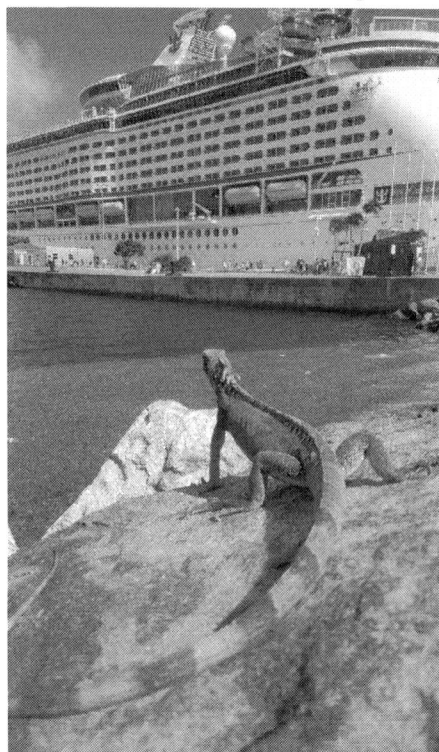

Should it be required, be prepared to book and pay for the first "audition cruise" as a first-timer if you are asked to. Once you have been contracted for your presentations, the corporate company websites will give you clues to the itineraries and timings of sailings (see the Appendix.) For specific dates and locations, go to an app like *CruiseMapper* to see where "your" ship is in the world, and see the relevant itineraries and dates for your booking. Take special note of the boarding and departure times, and especially that of the initial embarkation port.

CHAPTER 11
Here they are, at last, the Agencies!

Agencies may change, so more may be found online, but here are a few that you can start with, and may be all you will need.

- **Compass Speakers and Entertainment, Inc.** Ft. Lauderdale, FL, USA info@compassspeakers.com (954) 568-3801 www.CompassSpeakers.com With 27 years in the industry, the contact for high-end company positions. See the interview that follows for more specifics.
- **Sixth Star Entertainment and Marketing**: www.SixthStar.com; info@sixthstar.com or (954) 462-6760 □ **Posh Talks**: Palm Desert, CA U.S. www.Poshtalks.com; (619) 323-3205
- **Peel Talent**: Also offers training courses for aspiring cruise ship speakers, destination speakers and port lecturers www.theatreatsea.com; info@peeltalent.com UK: +44(0)1756 692506 www.CruiseShipSpeakers.com Speakers@peeltalent.com
- **EventzSpeakers**: for the Asia Pacific region for Special Interest Speakers www.EventzinParadise.com 61401183-4357 AU, NZ, S.Pacific, SE Asia

So, there you have it: the essential elements of securing free cruise ship travel while sharing your expertise, experiences, talents, and skills, along with what to do and who to call.

The cruise world is a mixture of nationalities and cultures, and this is your way of bridging the gap between nations. Communication, sincerity, and being of service makes all the difference in this tumultuous world. This is your chance to do your part to bring us together! Let's "teach the world to sing in perfect harmony!"

CHAPTER 12

Straight from the horse's mouth

An Interview with Andrew Poulton, Director of Outreach for Compass Speakers (6/2025)

Compass Speakers is a booking agency in Florida for high-end cruise lines with 27 years in the business. This interview will reveal the secrets of the requirements of an enrichment speaker.

Nancy: You have a distinguished position in the industry. From your vast experience, what is the most important thing that speakers need to know?

Andrew: Anyone who is serious about becoming a speaker on a cruise ship absolutely has to know their subject matter as an expert. They cannot just pretend to know their subject and say, "Oh, I've read articles about it, I've heard podcasts on it, so therefore I can speak about it." That doesn't work, because cruise ship passengers, especially, with the luxury cruise lines, are people that are well- educated, well-traveled, very knowledgeable people, and they're not easily fooled. So, the person has to be a true expert, and not just a fan of something or does something as a hobby. That's not going to work. They do have to be real experts.

Then, the second thing is, they have to be experts on subjects that are of interest to the audience. For example, I had someone the other day who proposed a bunch of talks on algae. Well, that's going to be of zero interest to a cruise line audience; another one was the history of golf. Well, again, unless it's a golf cruise, you know, nobody's going to be interested, or just maybe a handful of people, so the subject matter has to be of broad enough interest that enough people will go to the talks. It's kind of common sense, but you'd be amazed how many people are delusional about their knowledge or ability. A lot of our speakers are retired university professors or teachers. They're retired ambassadors, they're authors, they're experts in whatever field they were in for most of their careers. Most of them have had decades of experience in the matters that they're speaking about.

So, what I'm saying is that people really need to be serious before they go through the process of applying to be a speaker onboard a cruise ship. If they think it's just a cheap way of taking cruises, you know, they're very much mistaken; they have to prove themselves. And we have a pretty strict process by which we vet speakers. They have to submit not only their lecture titles, but also footage of themselves speaking. They obviously have to have the proper experience in whatever field it is that they're hoping to speak on, and it's a fairly lengthy process, and very thorough. Not all agencies, by the way, go through the same process that we do. Some just throw someone's information up on a website, and you're supposed to take it as truth. And some of the cruise line hire people on these sites, and they often regret it, because the caliber of people on these sites don't always fit the description. We only qualify a small percentage of the people that apply to be speakers. Like I said, our process it thorough and our people are professional.

Nancy: How long would it typically take for an applicant to be assessed as to their qualifications?

Andrew: Well, it can be as quick as the candidate wants. I mean, if they're willing to submit all the materials in one email, you know, we ask for things like a list of their books, their CV, a bio, and their passport information. They fill out an application form, and they provide footage of themselves speaking. So, if they have all that at their fingertips, there's no reason why they cannot submit it immediately and then be contacted within a few weeks. Some people take much longer because they don't have all the information, or they only have some of it back and forth, then it could take several months. So, I mean, we're not in a rush to do anything.

Obviously, we're always looking for good new speakers, but we're not pressuring to get people approved. We have our way of doing it, which is thorough and detailed. Once we get to the point where we qualify them, then there is an interview, which typically lasts about half an hour. That's what I do. That's my responsibility. Once these people have all their information, I go over their information, and then if I feel that they would be a good fit, then I set up another phone interview with them, and that typically lasts about half an hour. And it's for me to verify my initial determination of how eligible they are to be a Compass speaker. I'm just really making sure that that person is who they say they are, and they have the knowledge and experience to become one of our speakers.

Once they're re approved, it could take a year before they get their first assignment, because we, we work six to eighteen months out in terms of planning. We've already pretty much filled all our spots for 2025, and now our bookers are looking for 2026. Of course, there's always some chance that there's a last-minute opportunity, but typically it's six to eighteen months out. If someone gets approved today as a Compass Speaker, it's quite possible that it will be a year before they get sent out on a on a cruise ship.

Nancy: So, are you the ones that are placing them, or do the onboard managers from the ships tap into a portal and choose on their own?

Andrew: We are the ones that assign; we book it. We have some ladies who do the bookings, and they deal with the cruise lines, and cruise lines provide them with openings on upcoming cruises. Then they go through what the request was from the cruise line for what subject matter, and depending on the itinerary of the cruise, it could be very different. And then they go through our roster of speakers, and they decide which of the speakers would probably be most suited to that opening. They contact the speaker, and the speaker has to commit to that assignment. You know, often they can't because they've got another assignment, or they've got something personal that would preclude them from accepting it. So, it's a process. It takes a while. But like I said, we do things professionally and thoroughly, and we don't just throw people out there and hope they'll do a good job.

Nancy: Which cruise lines do you work with?

Andrew: We work with 10 cruise lines. They're all of the upper end of the of the cruise industry. So, we work with Crystal Cruises. Sea Dream, Azamara, Regent Seven Seas, Oceana, SilverSea, Viking, Cunard, Windstar and Paul Gauguin. So, we don't work with the mass market cruise lines like Princess, Holland America, Carnival, Royal Caribbean, or Celebrity.

We only work with the smaller and the more luxurious ships, kind of at the top end of the market. They are the lines that typically value the speakers more. For example, Viking's "Enrichment Program" is very important to them, so they insist on having the best speakers, and they take it very seriously. On some sailings, they may have three or four speakers. Most of the cruise lines typically just have one speaker, or sometimes two, if it's a longer cruise. They all want speakers, and they all feel it's an important part of the program, but some put more emphasis on it than others.

Nancy: Do those high-end lines require more of a time commitment and maybe tend to have longer cruises than the mainstream companies?

Andrew: Not necessarily. Most of Viking's cruise are seven days, but they do have some 10, 11, 14 days. And then some are longer, for example, Crystal and Regent have world cruises up to 140 days! So, typically, for a world cruise, the speaker will be on for anywhere from 10 days to two or maybe weeks. But once they've already covered their subject matter, they don't have that many talks for which they could stay on for longer.

Nancy: Sure, you've got the same audience. You can't keep repeating. Once you have determined that someone is qualified, is there anything that they would need to be aware of before they should accept an offer? Do they need to pay their own airfare to get there?

Andrew: No, generally the airfare is covered. However, they do pay a nominal booking fee to Compass Speakers. That's how we stay in business. So, they get to experience luxury cruising at a fraction of what they would have paid if they were a full paying customer, you know. It's a win-win situation for the for the cruise line, because they get these experts on board and they don't have to pay them; they pay the airfare for the speaker to get to and from the ship, economy class. And other than giving up the revenue for the cabin that they've allocated for the speaker, it doesn't cost them anything. So, it's a win for them. It's a win for the speaker, because, as I mentioned, they get to travel on luxury cruises for a fraction of the cost. And of course, it's good for Compass, because our name is out there and we get associated with some excellent speakers, and it's good PR for us.

Nancy: Who covers the costs of onboard gratuities?

Andrew: The speaker gets whatever passengers get. So, if it's an all-inclusive cruise line, like Regent, for example, gratuities are included. If they are not included and are additional like on Cunard, then the speaker needs to pay whatever is the recommended charge. So, the offering depends on the cruise line and what they offer their customers.

Nancy: Is there anything that a speaker needs to be aware of that they're not allowed to do, as opposed to being a regular guest on board?

Andrew: Well, we train our speakers to respect the cruise line and the authority of the cruise director on board, so our speakers know that they are not to be at the front of the line complaining bitterly about something. They know that if they haven't paid $1,000 a day, they probably shouldn't behave like someone who has. And, so if there's something wrong with the cruise, or if they have an issue, they are to contact the cruise director privately. And they shouldn't be out there complaining to other passengers about something. I mean, they're serving as an ambassador of the cruise line too. They're not employees of the cruise line, obviously, but they represent the cruise line as part of the program. So, it's a no-no to complain to other passengers or to be negative about the cruise line in any way.

But there are a lot of perks associated with this. They get whatever the passengers get. They sometimes like to put the speakers on shore excursions or tours to represent the company, so that way they can enjoy the tour without having to pay for it. That's a good perk. I mean, they're not the tour guide, but some of these excursions are very expensive.

Nancy: Oh, I know exactly! I've been sailing since 2011. I understand! So, if someone feels like they fulfill all of those requirements, that they have a good topic, they have availability, and they know how to behave, what is the best way to get connected? Do they apply through an online form, or do they contact you by phone? What's the best way for them to get hired?

Andrew: The best way for them to get hired is to go to our website at CompassSpeakers.com and to complete the application form online, which is pretty thorough, and give their background. Obviously, their basic details, like phone number, address, email, and all that stuff. But then they need to demonstrate that they are qualified in some way to even start the process. They can't just say that it's their hobby because that's not going to work.

And then the other thing is the subject matter, as I mentioned about the guy who wants to talk about algae, they need to put themselves in the shoes of their prospective audience, and ask themselves, "Is my subject matter something that would be of interest to an audience that's probably an average age about 65, very well-traveled, affluent, and educated?" "Do I have the right subject matter that would even interest these people?"

Now, the biggest demand that we have is for destination speakers, in other words, people that are true experts on the history and culture, and as well as the touristic highlights of the destinations that are going to be on the itinerary. If it's a Western Mediterranean itinerary, seven days say, Civitavecchia to Barcelona, they have to be experts on: the French Riviera, the Balearic Islands, the Spanish ports, the French ports, and the Italian ports. They have to really know their subject matter. But that's where the demand is. We get asked for destination speakers all the time, and we don't necessarily have enough of them. We love to recruit new destinations speakers because if they're good, there's a big demand for that.

If they have a very specialized subject, like maybe space travel or something like that, they might get hired to be on a longer cruise, where it may be a crossing, where there are no ports, and the cruise line is looking for a special interest speaker that can talk about something that's interesting but not related to the destination, there is some demand for that, but really the big demand is for destination speakers.

Nancy: I've heard that information about Cuba was a big draw. Is that still the case?

Andrew: No, because we were not allowed to go there anymore. Cuba opened during the Obama and Biden administrations, but you know, it's all been closed off now. So, no. US-based cruise lines are not allowed to go to Cuba.

Nancy: That's too bad. I'm grateful that I did get to go during that tiny window. Just proves you have to take advantage of opportunities as they may not come again.

Andrew: And I don't see any signs of that changing in the next few years.

Nancy: So, is the focus primarily on the Caribbean and the Mediterranean, or do you work in Asia or Africa at all?

Andrew: Yes. Our cruise lines are deployed worldwide. During the summer months, it's typically Alaska and the Mediterranean and Northern Europe. And then in the winter months, it's the Caribbean, South America, Asia, and Africa. So worldwide deployment.

Nancy: What ports do you have in Africa? I know some stop in Casablanca.

Andrew: Typically, mostly in the southern part of Africa, so Durban, Cape Town, East London. And then some of the cruises go up the west coast of Africa to Ghana, Namibia, and Angola, and some up the East Coast, to Madagascar, Tanzania, Zanzibar, and Kenya. And then, of course, when the Middle East is not in flames, there are Egypt, the Suez Canal, the Red Sea and all that. But obviously at this point, there won't be any cruises going through there for a while.

Nancy: I understand. World affairs are so changeable. Thank you so much for all that brilliant information and I will pass it along. There seems to be a variety of what's requested given the range of different levels of sophistication between different companies, and you provide a perfect conduit for opportunity.

Andrew: First of all, we've been in business 27 years, so we've been in business the longest as an established agency, and there's only a handful of agencies that provide enrichment, guest speakers to the cruise lines. So, there are a few others out there, but really, in my opinion, we are the most well established and most professional of those with certainly the most thorough process in the way that we vet speakers. We don't just, you know, throw them on a website and then get them to the cruise line. And I think we do a really good job, and our reputation is pretty stellar, I believe. And, you know, people aspire to be a Compass Speaker, and they get to go on some of the best cruises in the world.

Nancy: Well, thank you so much for your time, Andrew. This is brilliant. I really, really appreciate it, and I know the speakers will as well. It's nice to have somebody else's voice here besides mine, and this is valuable information straight from the horse's mouth, so to speak. Thank you so much!

So, there you have it! As you've discovered throughout these pages, the world of cruise speaking isn't just a fantasy—it's a thrilling, attainable path for experts like you who have something meaningful to share. Whether your passion lies in history, wellness, finance, travel, the arts, or any subject that sparks curiosity, cruise lines are actively seeking voices that inform and inspire. Imagine exchanging your knowledge for the chance to sail across turquoise waters, lounge on tropical beaches, explore legendary cities, and wake up to a new horizon—all without spending a dime on lodging or meals. This is more than a free vacation; it's a lifestyle upgrade that rewards your expertise with adventure, community, and purpose. So, pack your passion, polish your presentation, grab your passport, and step confidently into a world where your words can take you farther than you ever dreamed. The ship is waiting—and your story deserves a global stage.

Welcome to worldwide adventure!

Feel free to contact me at **nancysoule.author@gmail.com**

for pricing, timing, and details.

APPENDIX

Company	Number of Ships*	Guest capacity*	
CARNIVAL CORPORATION: www.carnivalcorp.com			1-800-CARNIVAL
Carnival	25	71,300	
Princess	14	42,000	
Aida	13	29,300	
Costa	11	50,713	
Holland America	11	25,900	
P & UK	6	18,600	
P & O Australia	3	8,200	
Cunard	3	6,700	
Seabourn	5	1,950	
ROYAL CARIBBEAN CRUISE LINES: www.Royal-Caribbean.com			305-539-6000
Royal Caribbean Group	28	94,700	
Celebrity	13	25,500	
SilverSea	6	4.916	
TUI	6	14,900	
NORWEGIAN CRUISE LINES: (owned by Star Cruises) www.NCL.com			305-468-2339.
NCL	16	46,600	
Oceana	6	5,200	
Regent	4	2,600	
OTHERS with smaller fleets:			
MSC	15	44,600	800-645-7270
Disney	4	8,500	407-566-3648
Azamara	4	8,500	online contact
Star Cruises (Hong Kong)	5	8,500	+86 2162720101
Hurtigruten (Norway)	6	6,700	888-966-4630
Viking	5	4,700	855-884-5464
Virgin	2	4,300	954 488 2955

*numbers as of 2023, and subject the constant updates with sales/scrapping of older ships and perpetual building of new ones in this multi-billion dollar industry.

About the Author:

Nancy Soulé is also the author of "Work at Sea, See the World", "Notes That Float," and a co-author of "For the Love of Transformation" with Hollywood's Roger Love. She is a speaker, musician, and founder of the Global Musician Academy: Notes That Float, helping musicians find a consistent paycheck while traveling the world. When she's not sailing (which is rare), she lives on an island near Seattle, Washington, and supports others who have ambitions see the world and share their talents. For book links go to Httsp://NancySoule.net. For the Global Musician Academy, see https://NotesThatFloat.net.

"Work at Sea, See the World: An Insider's Secrets to the Working Life on a Cruise Ship" (2023; Newman Springs Publishers. Available at Amazon and Barnes & Noble). Sailing consistently on cruise ships since 2011 as a musician, she is now a contractor/costumer for ship theatrical shows for ice, aqua, Broadway/West End, and corporate productions. She ship-hops, now being paid to sew and travel the world. For info on sea life, go to http://nancysoule.net

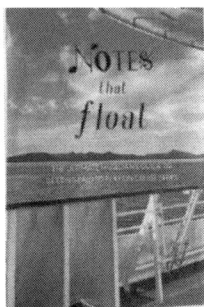

"Notes That Float: The Ultimate Musicians Guide to Getting Paid to Play on Cruise Ships" (2024; Amazon Publishing) This is the foundation for the online program, The Global Musician Academy, supporting ambitious musicians for consistent income and creative expression. This prepares them for the exclusive positions onboard and connection with hiring agents. For more information and a personal interview, contact MusicianSupport@NotesThatFloat.net to find out if you are a right fit for this floating city of international musicians, or find details at https://NotesThatFloat.net

"The Global Musician Program: Notes That Float
How to Land a Gig at Sea
This online program supports musicians' ambitions for consistent income and creative expression while utilizing their massive musical skills. It prepares them for positions onboard and connection with those who hire them. Nancy's passion is helping professional, ambitious musicians achieve positions on ships to get paid while experiencing the adventure of international travel and community. For information, see https://NotesThatFloat.net.

Scan this QR code or see http://nancysoule.net for more detailed information on all the books & programs.

Email: nancysoule.author@gmail.com or
Support@NotesThatFloat.net

Reviews, comments, and feedback are always appreciated!

Made in the USA
Middletown, DE
26 November 2025